The Turtle

Turtles are God's gentle little reminders to slow the pace, perhaps even stopping for a while to enjoy the journey. In American literature the turtle and the hare are in a race. The turtle runs the race slow and steady, eventually coming out the winner of the race against the fast paced hare. Perhaps the turtle is a winner in more ways than one. Let the *turtle of many colors* on the cover of your journal, be your gentle reminder to slow the pace, focus your thoughts and make discoveries within yourself along the path called life.

Whisperings

A Journey Inward, Discovering Your Own Unique Spirituality

MAGGIE JONES

WestBow
PRESS
A DIVISION OF THOMAS NELSON

ISBN: 978-1-4497-7332-8 (sc)
ISBN: 978-1-4497-7333-5 (e)

Library of Congress Control Number: 2012920384

WestBow Press books may be ordered through booksellers or by contacting:

WestBow Press
A Division of Thomas Nelson
1663 Liberty Drive
Bloomington, IN 47403
www.westbowpress.com
1-(866) 928-1240

Printed in the United States of America

WestBow Press rev. date: 11/13/2012

This journal contains my very deepest thoughts,
feelings and prayers. My journal is sacred to me.
Please do not read it without my permission.
Thank you for honoring my spirit and my privacy.

_____

Dear Friend,

Although I have not met you, I think of you as a friend. Jesus said, "I have called you friends" (John 15:15), teaching us perhaps to think of each other as friend. I have prepared this journal, prayerfully, just for you, in hopes that you might find a few moments during your week to seek silence and solitude with the Spirit of God, who lives inside of you. We live in a fast-paced, busy world. Your journal of *Whisperings* is meant to be counter-cultural to our busy world. Use your journal to slow-down, feel your feelings, touch the artist within you and nurture your prayer life. Let the Holy Spirit, our "Whispering God", speak to you through the art of journaling.

Your friend,

Maggie Jones

I have called you by name, you are mine (Isaiah 43:1)

Write your name as artistically and creatively as you can. Add as much detail, color and design as you like. When you have finished, take a few moments to admire your work, and hear God calling you by name.

Know God is smiling at the sound of your name.

My Birthday

I was born on:

in the year of:

And these are some things about me:

More About Me

My favorite things to do are:

Close Your Eyes & Breathe Deeply

The earliest memory of my life is when:

You Are The Author

Write a story about your life, beginning today.

Once upon a time:

You Are A Gift

What are the gifts or blessings that you bring to life. Remember, there's only one you!! The world is blessed by your life because:

Make It Happen

If you could plan your whole day, from sun-up till sundown, what would it be like?

Don't forget to describe the weather, what you would wear, who you would be with, what you would eat, where you would go and what would you do. Open all of your senses for this day!!

My Favorite Season

Spring?   Summer?   Autumn?   Winter?

What is your favorite season and what do you like best about this season?

At The Table

Several stories are written about Jesus eating with his friends. (Luke 10:38-42; Luke 22:14-20; Luke 24:30-35) We can know these meals were special gatherings, whatever the occasion. Each meal was special.

Who are the favorite people with whom you share meals?

Describe a memory of a meal that was special to you.

Making Jesus Personal For YOU!

Jesus asked the disciples, "who do you say that I am?" (Matthew 16:15)

Who do you say Jesus is? Name Jesus as your brother, shepherd, friend, Lord and Savior...whom?

Jesus is my:

My Fears

Make a list of your fears. Do not be afraid to name them.

What's Puzzling You?

Write about the parts of your life that you don't understand (include your home life, school, relationships, personal matters, illness)

The Wisdom Of All Ages

If you could give a message of wisdom to the world, what would it be? A word, a phrase, a poem or a speech...what is written in your heart for the world to hear?

What Makes You Feel Warm and Safe?

What Makes You Feel Cold and Frightened?

Forever Young

Jesus said, "Let the little children come to me." (Luke 18:16, Matthew 19:14, Mark 10:14)

What do you want to keep in your heart that is childlike?

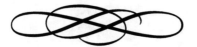

Part Of A Bigger Picture

What do I want to contribute to society?

What can I expect (what do I want) from society?

God's Blessings

What is God's greatest gift to you? What blessings do you receive from this gift?

Get Packing

What foreign country would you like to visit? Why? What would you want to do/experience there?

My Life's Creed

The creed we live by is our mission or code in life. It is a way of stating our intentions to fulfill our desired life results.

Write a sacred creed for your life. Write about your intentions, and commitments to each role you play in life as a daughter/sister, son/brother, friend…a beautiful creation of God.

By Land Or By Sea

If you could take a trip where would you go, the beach or the mountains? Why?

Whisperings Of The Spirit

Close your eyes and take a few deep breaths. Give thanks to God for your life. Listen to the Spirit of God that lives inside of you. If God wrote you a letter what might that letter say?

Dear _____ ,

A Letter to God

Write about your hopes, dreams, passions and fears.

Dear God,

Thinking Globally

My prayers for the world are:

Letting It Go

What do you want to be forgiven from?

Whom do you need to forgive?

It's A Metaphor

Write a poem about yourself using one, two or three words. Fill the page with your words.

I am like...

Meet My Mom

Write a poem about your mom, using one two or three
words per line. It's that metaphor thing again.

If you never knew your mom, what would she be like if you could imagine her?

My Mom is like...

Meet My Dad

Write a poem about your dad using metaphors.

If you never knew your dad what would he be like if you could imagine him?

My Dad is like...

"All Creatures Great and Small, Our
Lord God Created Them All"

– Cecil Francis Alexander

My favorite animal is:

How does this animal bring you joy?

Coming To Your Senses

Take a moment and thank God for the gift of your senses: sight, hearing, smell, taste, touch. Write a prayer of thanksgiving honoring your 5 senses. Be mindful of the fact, that there are those people that have lost one or more of their senses. Ask God to open the senses you possess in order that you may experience creation in its fullness.

Calming Storms

Jesus calmed the storm upon the lake. (Luke 8:22-25)

Is there a storm in your life? Is it a mild spring zephyr? Tornado? Hurricane? Thunderstorm?

Describe your storm.

Dream A Dream

I have a dream and it looks like this.

My dream is:

The Mystery Of People

Our world is a fabric sewn together with many people. We are all unique, making the fabric colorful, diverse and sometimes mysterious.

The biggest mystery about people is:

I don't understand why people:

I'm A Star!

If a movie were made about your life, what would be the title?

Would the movie be animated? documentary? foreign film with subtitles? drama? love story? mystery? What? Who would star as YOU in the movie?

Write the coming attraction announcement for your movie.

God Is Close To Me

I feel closest to God when:

God, Are You There?

I feel far away from God when:

Open A Door

See a door. With courage open that door and walk through it. What is waiting for you on the other side? Describe what is there.

My Door

Draw a picture of the door through which you walked. Include as many details as you can. You may want to give the door a name.

It's Working For You

Imagine you have been given an office in a large corporation. You are given the privilege of decorating the office in any way you wish or can imagine. What would your office look like? What will you put on the walls? the floors? the ceiling? What will you have on your desk?

The Corporate You

In what kind of corporation would you have your office? Describe the corporation where you have your office. What kind of impact does the corporation have on the world? the environment? Does it serve people? Does it receive from people? What role do you play in the corporation? Are you the owner? Name your company.

Imagine

You have decided to take a sailboat trip around the world with two other people (real or imaginary). The trip is half-way completed. With whom are you traveling? What is the name of your sailboat? Where have you been and what have you seen?

The Journey Continues

The sailboat comes upon a deserted island. You and your traveling companions explore the island for a day. Do you like the island and what have you found? Is the island lush and fertile? Or is the island a bit scary? barren? Do you decide to stay for a few more days and explore or do you want to continue your travels on the sailboat?

Ahoy Mate!

Name the island you have discovered. Draw a picture of your island.

A New Adventure

Your sailboat trip is completed. Now you are in a canoe paddling on a clear river. Describe what you see, hear and experience on this river.

Sit Back In Your Soul

My Soul is like...

Scripture

Read Psalm 121 in the bible. What does this verse mean to you?

Look To The Mountains

Draw the mountain in Psalm 121.

A Soul Map

Close your eyes and 'sit back in your soul'.

Draw your "soul map". Include anything you would like in it.

Mandala

Draw a circle. Draw something in the middle of the circle. Now continue to fill the inside of the circle with different shapes and designs until the entire circle is completed. Color your designs.

Song of Songs

Write a poem that sings the song of your life. If you could have someone famous sing your song, who might it be?

Step Into the River

Huckleberry Finn built a raft to sail the mighty Mississippi River. Draw a picture of your own raft, boat, canoe, yacht or ship.

Which river of the world would you put this vessel upon? Why?

Go Into The Desert

Lent marks the days leading into Easter. The bible tells us that Jesus 'retreated' to the desert to pray before his journey into Jerusalem. (Luke 4:1-13)

Spend some time with Jesus in the desert. The desert is sometimes seen as dry, and barren with little visible activity. What does your desert look and feel like? What would a journey into the desert be like for you? What would you take? What would you do?

Table Spirituality

Jesus ate with his friends on many occasions in the bible. The most special meal is described in the bible as the Seder meal or Last Supper. (Luke 22:14-20)

Create a meal for a special occasion. You are going to prepare all of the food. You are going to invite the guests. What would you serve to eat and drink? Who would you invite to be at your table? Where would you hold your dinner party?

A Capitol Idea

Imagine that you have been asked to design a Christmas ornament to be hung on the Christmas tree at the White House in Washington, D.C.

Draw a picture of your Christmas ornament. What does your ornament represent?

Especially For You

There is a gift for you under that White House Christmas tree. How is the gift wrapped and what is inside the package?

An Act Of Kindness

What is the kindest, nicest thing anyone has ever done for you? How did you respond to this act of kindness?

Giving Back

What is the nicest, kindest thing you have ever done for someone? How did they respond to your act of kindness? Did you realize how much your act of kindness would mean to that other person?

A Deeper Meaning

"You can never step in the same river twice."

What does this quote mean to you?

Heavy In Your Heart

The things that concern me the most are:

Name them all.

Color My World

If you could choose one color to paint your life, what color would it be? Why?

Self-Portrait

There is an artist inside everyone. Draw a picture of yourself. Don't be afraid of using abstract art.

Flower Child

A prayer for the day: Jesus thru your Spirit all life all goodness comes. I thank you for the spiritual bouquet bestowed on me. The bouquet I hold in my heart, for the rose to love and be loved; for the daisy that depicts the individual that I am. For the zinnia that blooms late into the summer; the beautiful old fashioned flower that can withstand the heat. The flower that says there may be others brighter, taller, more modern, but I have a uniqueness and everlasting beauty that makes me a favorite among many. I take my place in the yard and accept the beauty which I have been given by God.

Draw your favorite flower or create your own flower.

Those Around Me

Draw a picture of your family. Abstract is alright too.

Forty-Two Dreams

What are your dreams/desires for the world, yourself, your family?

The Love of Self

The love of self means to embrace the humanity entrusted to you by God. How are you true to yourself? How do you honor the child of God that you are?

Welcome To My Heart, A Place of Hospitality

A prayer for the day: Yahweh, I am your child. Open my heart to your love.

Draw a picture of your heart. Abstract is alright too.

Give It Three Days

Read the Passion of Christ (Luke 22, 23, 24)

Many things/events in life look differently after three days. Try and remember a struggle you have had in your own life that looked differently 'after three days.'

Or

Use this space to write about the next decision or struggle that arises. Wait three days and discover how it appeared then.

A Turtle of Many Colors

Design your own 'cover page' and create a turtle of many colors.

May You Be Blessed With Good Friends

May you learn to be a good friend to yourself.

May you be able to journey to that place in your soul where

There is great love, warmth, feeling and forgiveness.

May you treasure your friends.

May they be good to you, and be there when you need them most.

May you be good to your friends and may you be
there for them when they most need you.

May they bring you all the blessings, challenges, truth and light that you need.

May you always be in the gentle nest of belonging.

May you feel God's love through the friends given to you in life.

Author unknown